... *a compelling, must read* ...

"Kerryn's story is compelling and easy to read. Her journey through addiction, illness, despair and redemption leaves you amazed at how someone could not only survive, but thrive after such an ordeal.

Out of the Darkness not only tells of the downward spiral of the world of drug addiction, but also gives the reader hope that no-one is ever a 'lost cause.'"

Cathy Wieckmann (CHIPS Office Manager)

... *an inspiring story* ...

"There are many facets to Kerryn's story. In the main, it is the story of one woman's journey to 'hell' and back. From a childhood filled with love, Kerryn's life spiralled out of control after a casual experience with drugs. After many years of suffering, and nearly losing her life, Kerryn finally regained control when she 'gave' herself to God.

Kerryn's story not only shows the difference God has made to her life, it also provides a warning to all who think just one use of drugs won't hurt. Kerryn's story shows how much drugs can hurt – not just the user, but everyone around them.

This is an inspiring story – one that is hard to put down until the final page is read."

Rosalyn M. Dyne B.A. (Hons.)

... *will leave you amazed* ...

"Kerryn's book, Out of the Darkness, is not only an easy read, but one that will leave you amazed and inspired. A real eye opening story that is particularly good for teens and the parents of teens. I would go so far as to say this book may even change your life!"

Jason Kelaart B Bus & Com, Dip Bus, Cert IV Bus

... couldn't put it down ...

"*This is an awesome, must read. When I read a book, I often have trouble getting motivation to continue past the first page, but with Out of the Darkness I read it in one sitting. There was no way I could put it down. I had such an overall sense of excitement and anticipation of the hope at the end, the light at the end of the tunnel.*

Well done Kerryn! You are our walking, talking, transformed miracle and it is a pleasure to have you in our lives."

Alison Leonard   (Aged Care Activities Officer)

... strength and courage ...

"*Many people would see the ending of the Lou Reed song referred to in Kerryn's story as a natural law in life. Every action does have a reaction. We learn at school that every choice we make has a consequence. The choices that Kerryn made have been very hard ones to make, especially when we are so guided by society, trying to feel and be accepted by others around us.*

Everyone who reads this book will have empathy for the choices Kerryn made. She deserves every blessing for her strength and courage shown to all around her."

"*I am a little pencil in the hand of a writing God who is sending a love letter to the world. Let them find Jesus...when they come closer they have to choose.*" *Mother Teresa*

Michelle Nye B.A. Ed, Dip Ed. T.O.P.S

... a powerful story ...

Kerryn Redpath is a strong woman with a powerful story. Her book 'Out of The Darkness' was a great encouragement to me and is a great testament to the amazing grace and unfailing love of God. The courage and honesty Kerryn shares in the pages of her book will inspire you and give hope to people who are facing seemingly impossible situations. I am glad I read 'Out of the Darkness' and I love the way God has taken the mess of Kerryn's dark past and turned it into such a powerful message with such a bright future.

Justin Gardner
Senior Minister
Destiny Centre Christian Church
Author of *Crimeson*

... compelling, easy, must read ...

"What a compelling, easy, must read this story is. I read it in one sitting. I recommend anyone over the age of thirteen to read it, especially teenagers and young adults. It really demonstrates how the lure of having a good time can go oh, so wrong!"

Dani Cherrie author of *Pursued*

OUT *of the* DARKNESS

KERRYN REDPATH

Ark House Press
arkhousepress.com
Ark House Press, a division of Initiate Media.

This is a true story, only the names of people and places* have been changed to protect their identity.

Cataloguing in Publication Data:
Author: Redpath, Kerryn
Title: Out of the Darkness
ISBN: 978-0-646-53277-6 (pbk.)
Subjects: Drug addicts--Australia--Biography.
        Drug addicts--Rehabilitation--Australia--Biography.
        Drug addiction--Complications.
Dewey Number: 616.860092

Cover design and layout by initiateagency.com

To all who have lost a loved one to drugs
and
to those who are struggling with addiction

Forewords

I

Whether miracles happen or not, this story certainly reads like one. Diagnosed with a life threatening illness, Kerryn had virtually no chance of surviving. But Kerryn didn't know it. At her parent's request, those responsible for her medical treatment withheld the prognosis because they believed that if she knew, any hope, no matter how miniscule, would be lost.

I still clearly remember that Autumn day in 1982 when I first visited Kerryn in the Cardiac care ward at The Alfred Hospital. Somewhat naïve, I was amazed that a very attractive and obviously intelligent young woman should have such a serious, drug related illness.

I had met Kerryn in 1981 at her brother, David's wedding. Then, some twelve months later, I received an urgent call from David, advising me that Kerryn was suffering from a critical medical condition and he asked me to visit her. It was at this time that I began to realise just how serious the situation was. I happened to see her blood pressure readings. They were alarmingly high. Nobody, particularly the medical specialists really thought that Kerryn could possibly survive more than a very short time.

Amazingly, contrary to all expectations, Kerryn began to improve. But then came the bombshell. Complications developed and once again all seemed hopeless.

After many months of hospitalisation, Kerryn recovered enough to be discharged and tried to settle down to normal life. But there were many challenges. Often it seemed that her progress would be lost. After struggling like this for some years, Kerryn decided to explore healing in other ways.

Now 27 years later, despite many pressures, Kerryn lives a truly fulfilled life.

I hope that you will be as inspired by Kerryn's story as I have been.

Pastor Brian McKelvie

April 2009

II

This is a most compelling story which, in the context of tragedies associated with drug addiction, has a happy outcome. In her story, Kerryn describes her inexorable spiral downwards from a normal, loving adolescent, into the dark world of drugs and in particular, heroin addiction. She was one of the lucky ones. The dice never seemed to point absolutely directly at her. Her drug crazed world with heroin was brought to a crashing demise with the development of a severe infection (hepatitis B), which in turn led to a rare complication associated with this virus - polyarteritis nodosum. Death seemed inevitable, but with the intervention of appropriate medical therapy she rather remarkably survived. From that point, at almost complete rock bottom, she found a cause that was to set her on a lifelong rejection of the shattering world of drugs and addiction. This was catalysed by her new found beliefs in Christianity. To this day she remains well, both spiritually and physically, almost 30 years after her almost cataclysmic demise.

This is a story that should be read by all - young and old, parents, teenagers and current or past addicts of all persuasions. It is written in a simple matter-of-fact style. It is a story that should be especially read by all teenagers in their passage through the years of life, where they are most frequently brought in touch with the abhorrent world of drug addiction, in all its forms. This story strongly underscores the need for a faith in something (or someone) which provides the will and stability to reject this seductive lifestyle. In Kerryn's case it was her development of strong Christian beliefs in the power of prayer and God. She is a lucky one – she survived. This story is perhaps redolent of many, but nevertheless it is very compelling and provides a stark and sobering glimpse of the world of drug addiction.

Associate Professor Peter Ryan

2010

CONTENTS

Prologue

"He was gone. Here I was in the middle of the night by myself, with my dead boyfriend. What now? I could hardly breathe from the terror and the effort I had exerted trying to bring him back to life. Who do I call? An ambulance? There would be police! How could I tell his mother? I was crying, screaming, begging him to breathe..."

1

Innocence

My earliest memory is of my older brother, David and me sitting in a tin laundry tub, filled with water in our back yard. It was a steamy, Australian, summer's day in 1959 and I was nearly three and a half years old. Mum and Dad had moved to Melbourne from Shepparton, a country town in Northern Victoria, and bought a quaint little house in Richmond. Dad was planning to start a business in the city. David and I were both born in Richmond and spent our early years there. In January of 1960 we moved into a brand new home on a double block of land in Moorabbin. My parents had begun to fulfill the 'Great Aussie Dream' of building and owning their own home. In November of that year my younger brother, Ian, was born. I was a happy, much loved little girl with my older brother, David and younger brother, Ian. I always felt special as I was the only girl. We made good friends with Linda and Jenny over the road, Simon and James next door and then Steven, the Jewish boy who later moved in on the other side.

We spent the next few years living out of each other's pockets, often playing games that simply used our imagination. Linda, the eldest of the two sisters was a great story teller and filled our heads with many things that only an older sister would know. There were countless games of backyard cricket and in summer we rode our bikes to the local pool, with no helmets and sometimes even no brakes! Prior to Steven's family building on the block next door, we used to celebrate Guy Fawkes Night on the vacant land with a massive bonfire and an array of spectacular fireworks.

The winter months brought a whole new level of excitement. As we were only a short walk from the St. Kilda Football Ground, our neighbourhood came alive with the throngs of people headed for the Saturday matches. Linda and Jenny lived in a small fibro house on a large block of land. Every time St. Kilda had a home match the girl's family would make a tidy little sum, offering their entire property as a parking lot. We kids had the honour of collecting the parking fee and directing traffic. In my teenage years some girlfriends and I would watch the training sessions at the football ground, naturally interested only in the sporting side of the evening, not the young, fit, athletic, male bodies prancing around before us.

Every Sunday, my brothers and I were sent to Sunday School at St. David's Anglican Church, Moorabbin. A bus would come and pick us up, take us to church and then drop us off home again after the service. Mum and Dad didn't go with us; it was just the way things were done in those days. In light of this, the messages taught at St. David's were never discussed and church had no real significance in my life.

I attended Tucker Road Primary School from Prep to Grade Six, Moorabbin High for three years and then transferred to St. Leonard's in Brighton. It was a big, posh school by comparison, with its tennis courts, swimming pool and expanse of manicured lawns and gardens. I was fairly shy, being the 'new girl' but made friends quite easily and the girl I became closest to was Vicki.

From as early as I can remember I had a love of horses and rode other friend's ponies and horses until mum and dad finally bought me one of my own. He was a handsome chestnut gelding with a white blaze and I named him Tokay (a variety of red wine). Dad also bought a speedboat and after many hours of practice at various beaches and lakes, I became pretty competent at water skiing. As mum didn't ski and I was the only other female in the family, dad named the boat after me. That was embarrassing; my name was plastered across both sides of the boat in big block letters.

Most weekends were spent either horse riding, water skiing or hanging out with friends.

I have many wonderful childhood memories; in particular our Christmas holidays spent camping on Ulupna Island on the Murray River. We swam, skiied and swung into the water from 'Tarzan ropes' for so many hours each day that our skin would wrinkle. As I recall these times, I can still feel the burning heat of the hot sand on the soles of my feet and the painful sting of sunburn on my shoulders. Sunscreen wasn't around back then. Apart from our many encounters with spiders and a few with snakes, the scariest memory I have of the Murray River days was having to go to the dingy makeshift 'bush dunny', with its hessian walls and the hundreds of spiders that my imagination created. Sitting around a crackling fire on the beach and gazing into the brilliant starry heavens was often the peaceful ending to a long, active day. All of these things added to the excitement of our summer break. In later years, we changed our holiday destination to the Hume Weir Holiday Homes. Life was a little more civilized there, but we enjoyed many of the same activities plus nightly tennis matches.

Back home, with our school days spent together and our shared love of horses, Vicki and I became almost inseparable. Vicki already had a horse when I met her and after mum and dad bought Tokay, I moved him to the same agistment property, in Braeside, where Vicki kept her horse.

Later, Vicki's parents purchased a property at Pine Bay* and I was invited to move my horse down there. Pine Bay is a beautiful little sea-side town with two main beaches, a picturesque golf course with views over Westernport Bay and amazing horse riding trails. We began to spend every weekend at Pine Bay and gradually got to know the locals. It was at this time that I experienced my very first taste of evil: a taste that really shook my safe little world.

One afternoon, we had been hanging out with the local guys and a young girl from Melbourne, whom we had met a few times previously. Later that day this young girl headed back to town and that was the last time anyone ever saw her. That same night she was picked up in a car by some guy and brutally raped and murdered. He then dumped her body on Brighton Beach. A police van was set up in Pine Bay for a couple of weeks and police questioned many of the locals. Eventually the murderer was caught by police and jailed. He hadn't known the young girl; he had merely been an opportunist from Melbourne who spotted her walking along the footpath and enticed her into his car. That poor young girl was simply in the wrong place at the wrong time. What a tragedy!

At about 16 Vicki and I decided to do something daring by trying smoking. We got our hands on some cigars and hid in a stable at the horse agistment and coughed and spluttered, enjoying not the foul taste of the cigars, but the sweet taste of rebellion. We started to go to dances and sneaked a bit of alcohol whenever we could. This gradually slipped into regular smoking and drinking, especially when we went to dances, parties and pubs with live bands.

I think the first time I tried marijuana was at 18 when another girlfriend Kathy and I, drove to Lorne for a week. While we were there, we met a few guys who shared some joints with us. We thought we were just normal teenagers having a bit of fun.

After leaving school I began my first job in the Commonwealth Bank. I had a six month position at the Staff Training Centre in Melbourne and was then transferred to the Bankcard Centre. I was involved in mailing out Melbourne's first ever credit cards. What a curse!

Eighteen months or so later, I'd had enough of the Bank and found a new position as secretary/bookkeeper/receptionist for a small ceramics/kitchenware company in Moorabbin, where I saved as much money as I could. Vicky and I had begun to plan a trip overseas. At first, it was to be to New Zealand, but then Vicki was inspired by another friend's travels to India and Asia and our plans were changed.

The idea was to fly up to Kathmandu in Nepal and then gradually work our way back down through Asia to Malaysia, Indonesia and then home. We had allowed six to eight months for our big adventure.

2

Kathmandu

After months of planning and anticipation, hours of flying, a stopover in Bangkok and again briefly in India, Vicki and I finally arrived in Kathmandu. We were greeted by a surge of moist, hot air as we descended from the plane onto the tarmac. It was 1976 and security was pretty slack, so the check-out was quick and we soon found ourselves wandering around the streets of this amazing ancient city. One of the first smells we recognised as we meandered along, was the strong, pungent but familiar aroma of marijuana smoke. My fateful trip to Kathmandu had begun.

Our first place of accommodation was in a little lane named Pig Alley, in a run down two-storey, mud brick building. It was pretty rough, but fascinating, just what we Aussie back-packers were looking for. After a couple of days we moved to another place, which was even more dodgy, but closer to the centre of town. It was in the middle of Freak Street, where all sorts of activities took place right outside, all night, every night. This building had such a low roof that, being reasonably tall, I had to duck my head to pass under the ceiling beams.

We did some normal touristy things during the day, but most nights we seemed to end up in some sleazy 'smoking den' where pipes and joints were passed around and much hashish was smoked. The dens had a feel all of their own, with their colourful eastern-style fabrics draped about, and visitors sitting on cushions scattered around small tables on the floor. The lighting was dim and the room constantly filled with a thick haze of smoke, as we gradually numbed our minds with hash. Then, without warning, my adventure began to take a turn.

Within a week of arriving in Nepal, I became violently ill with vomiting and diarrhoea. It was fortunate that the bath was right next to the toilet as I was able to sit on the loo, while I threw up continually into the bath! After a few days of this, and despite how I was feeling, we journeyed on, travelling by bus to Pokhara; a magnificent, picturesque part of Nepal where we could easily see the peaks of the Himalayas early in the morning, before they disappeared into the cloud cover. We truly were in another world.

But I was becoming weaker. I pushed on thinking that I probably just had a bad dose of dysentery and treated it as such. Although I was seriously 'unwell', I kept hoping that it would pass and we continued on with our plans. After a week in Pokhara, we arrived back in Kathmandu, stayed a few more days and then caught a plane to Burma.

The next episode of our adventure was to travel by boat down the Irrawaddy River from Mandalay to Pagan. We caught a rattling, over-crowded train from Rangoon to Mandalay, spent a day there and then boarded the boat to begin our journey along the river to Pagan. This boat was actually some big, old ship and we paid for a shared cabin. Meanwhile, every inch of the deck was covered with locals who claimed a small space and sat or laid in that space for the entire voyage. Along the river, the towns and the people we passed were fascinating. At each town hoards of people lined the shore next to the ship hoping to sell their fruit, vegetables and wares to the passengers. But for me the whole journey was heart breaking, as in the midst of the extreme heat and humidity, my illness laid me useless. About mid journey our weary old ship ran aground and we were stuck in the one place for a whole day until the tide had risen enough for another passing ship to nudge us off the river's floor. I felt sooo sick!

We finally arrived in Pagan. It was a small but beautiful village with horse and buggy transport, dirt roads and gorgeous bamboo and timber huts. I did my best to enjoy this amazing part of the world, but it was there in Pagan, in the middle of one night, that I experienced my first episode of delirium. I had got up out of bed to go to the toilet and was feeling confused and disoriented. I sat down, leaning against a palm tree, my head spinning. I don't know how long I stayed there, but I knew things were not good. By this point I realised that my illness was pretty serious and as painful and disappointing as it was, I knew that I needed to head back home. I figured that if I wasn't going to survive, it would be better to die in Australia, rather than have my body flown home from Burma. What a bummer! I had planned six to eight months of travel and only lasted about a month.

Sadly, I left Vicki behind to continue 'our' trip alone and flew back to Singapore. My illness seemed to come in waves so I had moments when I could function reasonably well. In Singapore I met an English guy, who showed me around for a few days, before I caught my connecting flight back to the 'land of Oz'.

3

Home Again

I arrived back in Melbourne to be greeted by my family and the boyfriend I had left behind. I saw my doctor who assumed that I had contracted a severe dose of dysentery and prescribed medication to ease the symptoms. After a few weeks I began to feel much better and although totally disappointed about my abruptly ended travels, I resumed living my normal life.

I decided it was time to move out of home and I found a bungalow to rent from a lovely older lady down at my favourite hangout, Pine Bay. Daisy was a tiny lady who had been widowed for many years and she became like another mother to me, cooking for me and fussing over me. We shared many hours deep in conversation as she told me about her life and family and the years gone by.

One day, about three weeks after my return I was asked to help round up some cattle on horseback. Having ridden for years, I jumped at the opportunity. I saddled up one of Vicki's horses (my thoroughbred would have been too silly) and joined Jack and Rachel early in the morning to begin the round-up.

Jack was Rachel's father and a real personality in the township. He was a ruggedly handsome man with a shock of dark hair swept back from his face. Jack had worked for years as a professional fisherman and later drove the pilot boat out to the tankers when they were entering or leaving Western Port Bay. But Jack's greatest love was for his three children and he showed this by joining them in all of their leisure pursuits. Rachel was a slim, attractive young woman with long, dark hair. She was an extremely gifted horse rider and excelled in every discipline of the equestrian field, from dressage to showing and jumping and was even Female Jockey of the Year at one time.

We herded the cattle across a few paddocks and then slowed to a walk and moved them quietly out onto the road, heading in towards the Pine Bay township. It was a beautiful, crisp morning and all was going well until suddenly, a motorbike came flying around the bend toward us. The cattle instantly took fright and spun around, charging back in our direction. With the whole herd racing straight at us, my horse freaked out and spun on the spot, losing her footing on the bitumen. She crashed to the ground crushing my left leg under her full weight. An agonising pain shot from my foot up the length of my leg as I fought to hold back tears. I knew something was broken.

After a very bumpy ride to the nearest doctor, in Hastings, my injured leg was x-rayed revealing a 'Pots Fracture' just above the ankle; in other words both the Tibia and Fibula were broken and I was told my leg would be in plaster for the next six to eight weeks.

I continued to live in Pine Bay hopping around on my crutches. I was lucky that it was my left leg that was broken as my car at the time was an automatic and I was still able to drive. I was feeling quite well until about six weeks after arriving back from Nepal, when I awoke in the middle of the night in a complete delirium, totally unaware of where I was. By morning the delirium had passed, but I was not well. A girlfriend took me to Frankston Hospital, where I waited for several hours in the casualty ward, with my face bright red and my tongue white. I felt like I was dying. It was a Saturday and they were busy and I guess not expecting any exotic diseases to appear. I was finally seen by a doctor, had a blood test and was sent home. I went back to my family home in Moorabbin. No results were ever known from that blood test.

Once home my condition worsened. My family doctor made a home visit and this time diagnosed me with acute malaria and called an ambulance to have me rushed straight to Fairfield Infectious Diseases Hospital. I was admitted into an isolation ward, where my room was a six-sided 'cell' with barred windows. I was not allowed to leave the room and any visitors had to 'gown and mask up' before entering the room.

The next few weeks were just a blur to me. I have small windows of memory, such as when my mum, who visited every day, told me that they had finally, formally diagnosed me with 'Salmonella Para Typhoid A'. My earliest memories of that time consisted of feelings of extreme heat, extreme cold and my body being flopped back and forward as I was being sponged down. I was so close to death with my life just hanging in the balance. There was no sure cure for typhoid other than antibiotics and continually trying to keep me cool. I remember one instance when the nurses told me that I had been burning up with fever, but because my body was fighting it, I felt freezing cold. In an attempt to bring my extreme fever down, they tricked me by offering to give me a warm sponge. I agreed to that. Instead, they gave me an icy cold sponge and in my delirious state, I believed it to be warm.

When the delirium stage had finally passed and I was heading out of danger, I recall looking out of my window toward a huge palm tree, which reminded me of the tropical land I had recently left. I dreamed of being back there with Vicki, experiencing all of the awesome new sights and cultures instead of being trapped in this small, depressing 'prison cell'. Although I was happy for Vicki, the letters and postcards I received from her only magnified these emotions.

Some years later when talking to my mum about my five-week stint in Fairfield Hospital, mum, very surprised, corrected me -- I had been in there for ten weeks! I was stunned, but the dates she related proved her correct. I had been so sick that I had lost five weeks of my life. I had actually had my Typhoid vaccination before heading overseas, but I had contracted another strain of Typhoid, (para-typhoid) which the shots did not cover.

On Friday 13th August 1976 I 'celebrated' my 20th birthday in Fairfield Infectious Diseases Hospital with Salmonella Para Typhoid 'A' and a broken leg.

4

Wild Days

As soon as I was well enough, I moved back to Pine Bay and following a few months in my little bungalow, I moved into a small rental home with one of the local girls, Meg. She was an intriguing young woman with many friends and a very creative side. Meg was tall and slim, with a model-like body and a beautiful face with well shaped cheek bones, but she was really into drinking, smoking dope and partying. Naturally, I joined in and gradually slipped deeper and deeper into the drug scene. The next drug we both discovered was 'magic mushrooms'. These have a very powerful hallucinogenic effect and as they grew in abundance locally we used them regularly. At first, the mushies were so much fun. In fact for a while there, we never wanted to come down off them, but after a time their effect began to change.

At this time, Meg and I were working at a local poultry farm. One day, after another night of magic mushies, we both woke up with weird physical side-effects. My thumbs weren't working properly. It was as though they had no bones in them and picking up eggs at work was extremely challenging. Meg found that her legs had become very weak and kept collapsing on her. We decided that perhaps we should have a break from the mushies and we did, for a week or so. But these were not the only side-effects. After a while the 'trips' were not always as much fun. Meg in particular had quite a few bad trips. Her mother, who was a very kind woman with a gentle soul, had been a tarot card reader and she had had five nervous break-downs. Years later I came to understand the significance of this.

One night things really turned bad. We'd had a few friends around and all of us had smoked dope and taken 'mushies'. After our friends left to go home both Meg and I went to bed. The doors to our rooms were at right angles to each other. It was late and I lay in bed trying to sleep but was not having any success as the drugs in my system were keeping me awake. All of a sudden my door began to open. The silvery moonlight streaming through my window gave me a clear view. Staring straight at me was a tall, terrifying half man, half dog with bright yellow eyes. I guess you would call it some sort of werewolf. I was absolutely frozen with fear. I held the sheets up to my face and my breathing stopped. It seemed like it was there forever, but then it moved back, pulling my door shut with it. I breathed again. About 30 seconds passed and the house was suddenly filled with blood curdling screams from the room next door. 'It' had gone into Meg's room.

Fear filled every inch of my being. I had two choices. The first was to head for the front door and run for my life. But that could be disastrous. We were in the bush and it was night time. My second option was to run into Meg's room and help her to fight off this freaky, grotesque creature. I opted for the second choice. I raced into the room next door only to find that Meg had also seen this terrifying creature and was now having another completely different experience. Meg was hysterical, convinced that someone was being stabbed to death in our front yard. I heard nothing. We eventually managed to calm each other down and went back to bed. The following morning there was another strange, random event. Both of our dogs were vomiting, with no obvious explanation. I don't know what that was about but there was no doubt, there had been a very dark, heavy presence over our little house that night.

Despite this ordeal, the partying continued. At one point I told some guys I knew, about the experience of that night and they said that it sounded like I had seen Satan. I laughed.

Some time over the next few months another friend admitted to me that he had been using heroin. I had been curious about trying heroin and asked if he could get some for me. We arranged a date and I had my first taste of heroin. It only had a very mild effect on me. I think I was either a bit ripped off, or he was just being cautious not to give me too much. This only made me more curious and before long I found other contacts and began to 'use' more regularly. Heroin is one of those drugs that kind of sneaks up on you. I never intended to get hooked; it's just that once it gets into your system, you begin to crave the euphoric feeling more and more. It's like the mental addiction kicks in before you actually have a real physical addiction.

5

In Too Deep

After three years of living in Pine Bay I decided to move back to Melbourne. Soon after, a friend invited me to a fancy dress party in South Caulfield. My dear Grandmother had just passed away and I had to drive to Shepparton and back that day for her funeral. On my return, I changed into my costume and headed to the party. Now, dressed as a cowgirl, with my eyes puffy from crying, I was a bit of a mess. David R was the host of the party and he showed me a lot of attention that night. He was a pretty cool guy, very intelligent and creative and I felt drawn to him too.

We soon began a relationship and life was amazing. David R was very loving, attentive and protective of me and he showed me the fun things and culture of city life: a huge contrast to my three years in the country. David took me to concerts, street festivals and restaurants. Our favourite dining place became an Indian restaurant in Chapel Street, Prahran, called the 'Taj Mahal'. He even took me to an opera, 'La Traviata'. I think his mum shouted that one. But there was also the dark side. I had been using different drugs for a few years now and David was well and truly into heroin. I saw this as another bonus as I had really developed a taste for heroin and he had the contacts in Melbourne. I continued to drift into this forbidden, but enticing world with no idea of where it would lead.

I began an office job at a large company importing musical instruments in South Melbourne and before long, moved in with David. Our lives became a world of work, drugs, alcohol and parties. As well as heroin, or smack as we called it, we often used speed, a drug which kept us awake for hours or even days at a time and took a terrible toll on our bodies.

David also joined the company I was working for in South Melbourne and as it was very close to Fitzroy Street, St. Kilda, where we scored our drugs, we often called in on the way home and did just that. Even worse, many times we slipped out at lunch time, scored heroin and either hit up in a local park, or we'd go back to work to have it. David would have his hit in the toilets downstairs and then buzz me on the intercom. I would then go down and collect my share (which David had mixed in a syringe) and take it to the toilets near my desk and have my hit. I'm not sure if anyone ever caught on. Possibly not, as this was a company with a culture of long lunches with excessive alcohol consumption. However, when I think of it now it makes me shudder to imagine what would have happened if one of us had overdosed in the toilet cubical at work.

To a person who has had nothing to do with drugs, this behaviour might seem unbelievable, but believe me, for anyone who is involved in drugs, this is just the way it is. The more that you use, the more you begin to slip down the slippery slope, without really being able to see how far you have fallen.

As I recall all of these memories, I just want to pause to say... I am not proud of any of this. I'm just telling the story, as it was, in the hope that anyone reading might come to recognise the pain, suffering and hopelessness that drug use brings. If I could turn back the clock and change any of this to erase the heartache and pain this later brought to me and my family, I would do so in a heartbeat. As I indicated previously, I was brought up in a loving, supportive family and was really quite a shy and very straight young girl, all through my teenage years. But I made one huge mistake and opened the door into the dangerous world of drugs. Once this door had been opened, I entered into a bizarre, abnormal world that eventually just became like normal for me. Even though I knew that this behaviour was illegal, my judgement had become blurred and the lie of 'this is ok' became as truth.

One day, out of the blue, David and I had a visit from a few guys whom we knew, but were not close to. They had come with some smack (heroin) to sell. Naturally we took up the offer; they came in and we all sat around and indulged together. They stayed for an hour or so. After they left David and I commented that they had seemed to be looking around, 'casing' the place while they were there. Sure enough, about a month later, it happened. We came home from work one day and found the front door wide open. My dog Mandu, who should have been in the back yard, was sitting on the front porch, wagging her tail and 'smiling'. So much for our watch dog! I felt sick in the stomach as I realised what had happened. While we had been at work, our home had been broken into and both our T.V. and Hi Fi system (and a few other possessions) were stolen. We reported it to the police, but naturally could not inform them of our suspicions as that would also implicate us.

About six months later, I had a call from the local police informing me that officers in a police helicopter had spotted three young men breaking into another home in the area. The three were caught, arrested and taken to the local police station where they were questioned. They admitted to committing thirteen house burglaries including the one at our home. I asked the officer if he could tell me the names of the offenders and he obliged. Sure enough, they were the same so-called friends who had visited us and 'cased' our home a few months earlier. Of course I could not say that I knew any of these guys as once again this would implicate us. The sad truth of this story is that when drugs are involved, people get desperate and friendship lines are crossed without a second thought.

☞

When David and I had been together for about a year I accidentally fell pregnant. As this was unplanned, and we were both heavily involved in drugs, we decided to have the pregnancy terminated. I attended a clinic where the compulsory counselling consisted of a five minute session. What a joke! It was too easy and tragically, years later, David said that he only agreed because he thought that was what I wanted. Sadly, I thought it was what he wanted. At the time I had no idea that just a few years later, I would desperately regret this decision.

There are so many horror stories involving drugs and we were not immune to them. Overdoses were the most common tragedies of this lifestyle and when we were with friends using drugs, it was not unusual to have someone O.D. and to see someone else come to their rescue with mouth-to-mouth resuscitation. I didn't ever actually see anyone use heart massage. Once again that was just the way it was. I happened to O.D. three times and each time David resuscitated me.

One such incident stands out in particular, because of the reaction of a guy called Tony, who was with us at the time. We were in a flat in St. Kilda where we had divided up some smack and all had our 'hit'. Afterwards, I lit a cigarette and accidentally dropped a box of matches on the floor. I leaned down to pick them up and didn't come back up again. I had O.D'd. Of course I remember nothing of the next few minutes, but suddenly I found myself lying on the floor with a wet face, and Tony was jumping up and down almost crying at the sight of me regaining consciousness. He had been terrified at the sight of me unconscious as David battled to get me breathing again. Apparently I had been gone for a while and David had given me mouth-to-mouth resuscitation while Tony tipped a glass of water over my face, in an attempt to resuscitate me. We really were playing with fire.

That was not the only 'lucky' break I had. One night a really amazing thing happened. David and I had been for drinks at a local South Melbourne pub with work mates to celebrate either a birthday or someone leaving and we both drank far too much. On our way home we were craving a hit, so we stopped off in Fitzroy Street and scored. We were renting a 100 year-old-house in South Caulfield at the time (where the fancy dress party had been held) and a friend, Liam, was renting a room with us. As we were both so intoxicated and had also used heroin (a very dangerous mix) I went into Liam's room, fell into the armchair he was in and asked him to check on us later because of the dangerous cocktail we had had. I left his room and headed back to ours with the intention of lying on the bed with David to watch T.V. I woke up nearly three hours later, lying on the floor of our room! I had collapsed before reaching the bed. Liam, who had also been drinking, fell asleep and never came in to check on us. To collapse like that and not die was unbelievable... someone was watching over me.

We knew of friends who did succumb to the drugs and it was always a shock to learn of their death. Another young life tragically wasted and yet most people who used, still believed that it would never happen to them. Another big lie!

It may seem that drug O.D.s are not that big a deal as I have listed cases where others have managed to successfully resuscitate victims. However, nothing could be further from the truth, as many users O.D. alone or in a group of people who are also drug-affected and as a result, are unable to recognize that a person is in danger. The following scenario relates to one such tragic course of events.

A popular young man, whom I had met on one occasion, had been to a party with a group of friends where they had all used heroin. Later the group headed home in a car and on their arrival went inside. As they had all been affected by the drugs, they did not notice that their friend was still in the car. The following morning, to the horror and disbelief of his friends, the young man was found dead in the back seat of the car, leaving yet another grief stricken family to pick up the pieces. The problem was, the group of friends had been too 'out of it' to notice that their friend had O.D'd, which in turn meant that any possible chance of resuscitation was missed. Tragically, this happens all too often.

6

Terror

One of the most terrifying nights of my life began with a fun night out at the Crystal Ballroom in Fitzroy Street, St. Kilda. 'The Models' were playing and they were pretty big at the time. David and I and a few other friends joined a huge crowd in a packed, smoke-filled room and drank and danced the night away. At one point David said that he was going to the toilet and disappeared from sight. I was having too much fun to notice how long he had been missing and at the end of the night he was back with me and we headed home. I can still remember laughing and staggering arm in arm with a few friends down the street to our car. I had no idea of the nightmare that lay ahead...

We were living at Black Rock at this stage and we somehow made it home. By now I had the munchies and decided to cook up some muffins with egg, bacon, tomato and cheese and set about doing this. David said that he was feeling hot and sweaty from the overcrowded room we had been in and decided to have a shower. I merrily cooked away and when the food was finally ready I knocked on the bathroom door to let David know. There was no response, so I opened the door to stick my head in and call out a bit louder. The room was filled with steam. All David had managed to do was to turn on the hot tap. (What I didn't know was that while he had disappeared from the venue to 'go to the toilet' he had actually sneaked out of the venue and scored heroin.) I looked over through the thick mist of steam and there was David - naked and slumped over an old disused oil heater. I freaked. I raced into the bathroom and pulled David's limp body onto the floor. He was blue and his head hit the floor with a thud. I fell to my knees beside him to begin mouth-to-mouth but his jaw was clamped so tightly shut that I had to use all the strength I could summon to force his mouth open. I was in an utter panic. I had seen plenty of O.D.s, but I had never seen anyone looking so far gone...so dead.

I began to blow madly, furiously into his mouth over and over and over again. Nothing was happening. I continued on in a state of absolute terror for at least 15-20 minutes. Utterly exhausted and with no response from

David at all, I stood up realising that it was no use. He was gone. Here I was in the middle of the night by myself, with my dead boyfriend. What now? I could hardly breathe from the terror and the effort I had exerted trying to bring him back to life. Who do I call? An ambulance? There would be police! How could I tell his mother? I was crying, screaming, begging David to breathe.

My head was spinning and in a state of excruciating fear I fell back to my knees and desperately continued to blow air into his lungs, with every ounce of strength I could muster. Finally, after at least another 15 or 20 minutes, an eerie groan came from David's mouth. I breathed some more air into his mouth then shook him, slapped him and shook him again. At last, he began to regain consciousness.

Throughout the remainder of that night, every time David closed his eyes, I prodded him to make sure he stayed alive. I could not believe what had happened to us and just how close that had been. The memory of that night will stay with me forever.

For the next three days I could barely breathe, I had blown so hard and for so long in my effort to resuscitate David that my entire throat and windpipe area was red raw. You would think an ordeal like that would be enough to turn us off the drugs forever. Unfortunately not! As for David, well, he'd been unconscious the whole time and really didn't comprehend the severity of the O.D. I think he just thought he was so tough! And with him still using, how could I stop? It was so addictive. It's just not that easy.

7

Repercussions

We continued on with work, drugs, alcohol and parties until one night while we were dining out at a pancake restaurant in the City, I suddenly became extremely itchy all over my body. I had to go into the ladies room to strip off and scratch frantically. We headed home and the following morning I woke up with welts all over my body. I drove down to the local Sandringham Hospital where I was diagnosed with some sort of allergic reaction. I was given some antihistamines and sent home. Three days later the welts disappeared but I woke up stiff all over. This turned into a form of arthritis so my GP referred me to a rheumatologist who did a blood test which revealed

Hepatitis B. The arthritis lasted for three and a half months. Then the Hepatitis B symptoms followed. Although I had no jaundice, which I probably should have had, I was very lethargic and lost a lot of weight. I was given two months off work. At the end of that two months I was no better, so I was given a further two months off. Still the symptoms did not abate and unbeknown to me or to my doctor something else was going on inside of me.

Because of my sickness, I moved from the house that David and I shared to my parents' home. By this time I was fed up with being sick. When I heard of a party in Black Rock, I decided to take some analgesics and go out and enjoy myself. It was a bikie party and there was an abundance of alcohol and speed. So, feeling a bit better (because of the analgesics I had taken), I decided a little speed wouldn't do any harm and snorted a small line.

When using speed you tend to lose track of time. I'm not sure exactly when it was, but while I was in the backyard, suddenly a violent fight broke out between two girls. It was wild; biting, scratching, hitting, hair pulling and kicking, not to mention the language. A few people went to step in, but others said "Just let them get it out of their system," and the fight continued. After that, with all the drugs and tension in the air, just as suddenly, I witnessed another guy getting 'king hit' and as he hit the ground, a whole group of others laid into him. In my altered state of mind it was kind of surreal. I was watching it in silhouette as there was a bright spotlight behind them, and I remember thinking "What a pack of cowards", taking on one man like that.

I guess it was a couple of hours later when the host of the party (who had been the King Hitter) came up to me and asked "How is David"? I didn't understand until he explained that it was David who had been bashed. I demanded he look for him. I found David's sister and after frantically searching for a while, we headed home. David was there. He had staggered home and was trying to drum up some friends to go back for a pay back. The room was filled with tension as David's sister and I tried to calm him down.Suddenly, the back of my neck became stiff and I felt an agonising pain like the stab of a knife, and that was the last thing I remebered. Three days later I woke up in the Alfred Hospital. I'd had a Grand Mal seizure and David had tried to resuscitate me while his sister had called an ambulance. I was rushed straight to the hospital. Over the next couple of days I drifted in and out of consciousness as the seizures continued. My condition was assessed as a drug and alcohol overdose, although I had definitely had no alcohol and only a very small line of speed. (The assumption of alcohol came because David had been drinking and he had given me mouth-to-mouth resuscitation, leaving the smell of alcohol on my breath.) I was sent back home again, but the doctors were totally unaware of what was really going on in my body.

Over the next few weeks I became weaker and weaker. By this time the average Hepatitis B patient should have been improving. Mum took me to another doctor who did an ECG and referred me urgently to a specialist at the Alfred. I was to see him the following day. By this time even the least amount of physical effort left me exhausted and breathless. Mum had to drop me at the hospital door, where I slumped on the steps while she parked the car. The Professor (Professor Firkin), whose clinic I was about to attend, happened to walk by. On seeing the state I was in, he promptly ordered a wheel-chair to carry me to his consultation room.

I was quickly assessed and diagnosed with acute heart and kidney failure. Professor Firkin immediately called for a trolley. I collapsed onto the trolley and was raced through the hospital corridors to the Coronary Care Unit. At that point I was given less than two hours to live! In fact my family was informed that I could die "at any moment!"

A code blue alert rang throughout the hospital as the emergency doctors who were on call raced to my side. I was attended to and examined by the Alfred Hospital's top heart, kidney and immunology specialists who diagnosed me with a form of cardiomyopathy. They said that my only chance of survival would be to have a heart transplant, but I would need it within the next two hours. Of course it would be impossible to find a matching heart and set up surgery for such a complex operation in just a few hours.

But there was also another problem. My renal failure was so severe, that my kidneys would not withstand the surgery. I had less than five percent function of both kidneys.

In his attempt to break the shocking news to my mother, Professor Firkin said "Kerryn is in an extremely serious condition. We do not expect her to live!" He paused, then added "We cannot hold out any hope. This condition has a 99.9% mortality rate." My family quickly gathered around as I lay in the Coronary Care Unit (CCU) waiting to die.

I felt like dying. My heart was so enlarged that it was racing at about 300-400 beats per minute rather than 70-80 beats and because two major organs were shutting down, my body was filling up with fluid. As a result of this, I had pulmonary oedema; my lungs were flooding and I could barely breathe. My body ached all over and my blood pressure was sky high. I had huge lumps of fluid all over my body.

Because of the acute kidney failure, my fluid intake was severely restricted. I was deprived of the elixir of life... water...and I vividly recall begging for just an ice block or even a wet flannel to suck on, as thirst began to overwhelm me.

The room was filled with a myriad of monitors and machines. I had a blood pressure cuff permanently on, an octopus drip pumping different drugs into my arm, a urine catheter connected and an oxygen mask strapped to my face. I clearly remember that time as I gasped for every breath. It was as though the air could not quite reach my lungs and I pulled the mask off and on again over and over desperately trying to ease the excruciating discomfort. It felt like I was drowning. I recall doctor after doctor lifting my hands to look for signs of hemorrhaging or septic shock in my fingers, as they battled to keep me alive.

It was at this time that a brilliant young immunologist/rheumatologist (now Professor), Peter Ryan, was on duty and he managed to diagnose my condition. It had now been labelled 'Polyarteritis Nodosa' which translated means many inflamed arteries and nodules'. This had apparently been caused by some malfunction of my auto-immune system. Rather than fight the Hepatitis B disease, my anti-bodies had attacked my body and as this was a rare condition, it had not been picked up earlier.

There I lay, my life rapidly slipping away as my stunned and devastated family hovered around. I had always managed to hide my drug problem from them and now, not only had they just been informed by the doctors that this was all drug related, but they were about to lose me. What had gone so wrong? Where was the healthy, happy young girl they once knew?

My doctors were amazing. They administered many different drugs including high dose steroids and an immunosuppressive medication, called Cyclophosphamide, in an attempt to reverse the inflammation to my organs and arterial system. Approval had to be given from Canberra before this drug could be used. However, by this time the damage to my body was so severe, that to turn things around in just a couple of hours was 'out of the question' and this is just what my family was told. At the time, mum refused to let the doctors tell me that I was expected to die. She reasoned that not knowing, might give me the strength to fight on. I had no fight left in me at all. The only hope left for me would have to be a miracle. My family was told to pray.

❦

My older brother David had become a Christian some three years earlier and had tried to tell me about this Jesus bloke, but I had decided that this was not for me. Now, with his little sister critically ill, David, in desperation, contacted his church Pastor, Brian McKelvie, asking that Brian and other believers pray for me.

The prayers began. Miraculously, I survived the next few days and on my fourth day in the CCU, I was sent off to have an angiogram. The result was bad. The specialists informed my family that the damage to my body was so severe, that "nobody could possibly survive it." I remained in the CCU waiting to die.

❦

Meanwhile the prayers continued and on the seventh day my doctors were scratching their heads, wondering why 'this young woman' was still alive. I was sent off to have another scan of my heart and the following day the result came through. I had three different specialists visit me and their words were, "This is amazing." "That is not the same heart." "It's like you have a new heart." My heart was now miraculously beating strongly and had returned to normal size. I remained in hospital for nearly five months in a general ward while my kidney function slowly improved.

8

God?

Whilst in the general ward I encountered my first inkling of the possibility that there might actually be a God. I had not yet recognised His hand on my life, but one night as I lay in my bed I heard a terrible groaning coming from the next room. When a nurse came in to check my drip, I asked her what was happening. She probably shouldn't have told me, but they knew me well by now. She told me that a 17-year-old girl was dying from leukaemia next door. She said she was in the final stages and that she was not expected to live through the night.

I don't suppose anyone could imagine how I felt unless they had been in this situation. I could hear this young woman struggling for every breath as she was about to leave this world. In a state of sheer grief and desperation at the sound of her groans, I cried out from the bottom of my heart to a God I didn't know and asked Him to spare her. I told Him that I had caused my own sickness and deserved to die and that she did not - I begged Him to save her. I'm sure I was not the only one who was praying for her that night.

The next morning the ward was abuzz with excitement. Emily, my next door neighbour, had miraculously gone into remission during the night. The following day she was up and about, bald headed and pulling a drip pole on wheels around with her. Emily left the hospital before me and later called me to see how I was going. Unfortunately, I have since lost touch with her.

9

What Will It Take?

My stay in hospital was long and depressing. I was so sick and unbelievably thin and weak. I can still remember the first time that I actually stood up for an entire shower, instead of sitting on a plastic chair. Halfway through I began to shake all over, but I was determined not to give in and sit down. I made it!

Apart from some friends' visits and mum's daily visit, my brother's Pastor, Brian, came in regularly, which was really great for my sanity as he helped me to 'unload' some of the stuff that was spinning in my mind. Lying around for so many months, too weak for any physical activity, really messed with my head. I was, however, fortunate that I was blessed at birth with a positive outlook on life. Nevertheless, this was really putting my sanguine/choleric (optimistic/determined) personality to the test.

After about two and a half months in hospital I was allowed out for weekend leave. I went home and a friend came and picked me up and took me to her place for the afternoon. She and some friends had been smoking some bongs and I begged them to give me just a little smoke. They finally relented and I had a very small pipe. After a few hours I began to realise that I was far more stoned than I should have been and I started to panic. Suddenly, it really hit me that I had just had heart and kidney failure and that mixing dope with the medication I was on was pretty stupid. I lay down for a while hoping to recover, but this made no difference. I was in a really bad state and I asked my friend to drive me home. By this time I was totally spinning out and now I had to face my parents. They quickly drove me back to the hospital. No one spoke on that journey.

Once I had returned to my ward I had a blood test. The doctors wanted to check just what drugs I had taken. They didn't believe me when I told them that it was only a small amount of marijuana. And who would blame them? The next day, my head specialist, Prof. Firkin, came into my room with his tribe of student doctors and stood at the end of my bed. With his usual calm voice of authority he said, "Kerryn, God helps those who help themselves". He then spun around and marched out. I felt so small. That was the last time I ever used drugs.

A female specialist, who was also supervising my case, was so angry with me that she refused to talk to me. I don't blame her at all for that. My case had put my doctors under immense pressure as they agonised over balancing drug doses and combinations, all the while trying not to destroy my ovaries, just in case. Once again mum stepped in. She pleaded with my doctor to forgive me, saying that I knew I had messed up and that I needed all the support I could get to make it through this. Following this latest episode, I also had to see three psychiatrists to prove that I was actually sane. My doctors had been really excited as they had just managed to get a brand new drug - Interferon - in from Finland for me, at a cost of $80,000 to the Government. That was a lot of money in 1982. This drug had never been used in Australia before. They had to make sure that they were not going to waste it on someone who might just go out and O.D. Somehow I managed to pass the sanity test.

Interferon was used in an attempt to cure the Hep B, as while I still carried the Hep B virus, my antibodies could at any time re-ignite the condition which could again become potentially lethal. Interferon was still in the experimental stage and consequently, the dose I was given was more than I could tolerate. This caused me to vomit a number of times, throwing up the medication that was keeping my blood pressure down. As a result, my blood pressure rapidly increased and I began to have more Grand Mal seizures. The seizures were so violent that I fell out of bed, ripping a drip out of my arm. This time I fell into a coma. Once again a code blue alert rang throughout the hospital as all of the emergency doctors raced to my side. I was gravely ill in ICU; and much later Brian told me that by now he had begun to lose hope that God would heal me. Again my family rallied around preparing for the worst.

However, God had other plans. The prayers continued and after three days I awoke from the coma and my kidneys slowly began to improve.

During my stay in hospital, I underwent many different tests including a lumbar puncture, a bone marrow test, an angiogram, hundreds of blood tests and scans and one of the more memorable ones, a kidney biopsy. I was told this particular test should take about thirty minutes. But there was a problem. Both of my kidneys had been so severely damaged that they were small, shrivelled and covered in tough scar tissue. Apparently they were both about the size and appearance of a walnut. I was given a Valium drip to relax throughout the procedure so I didn't really notice the time that passed, although I do remember the doctor's anguish and frustration. My kidney damage was so severe that the procedure took three and a half hours and they were still not able to penetrate the tissue enough to get a sample from either kidney. What I do remember vividly was that for the entire procedure I lay face down with my arms above my head. At the end of the three and a half hours, my arms were locked in that position and this led to a very slow, painful process, as I tried to lower them down again. By this point my kidney function had reached approximately forty percent and that's where the improvement stopped.

10

The Love of a Mother

Nearly four months into my stay in the Alfred I was allowed out again for a day. Mum picked me up to take me for a drive and after spending such a long time 'locked up' and isolated from the outside world, going out felt really weird. I had become sort of institutionalised. The sterile environment, the smell of cleaning chemicals and the endless routines had become 'normal' to me and stepping out into the real world hit me hard. My senses were on high alert and the smells and sights of the city actually made me nervous. Everything was so loud and the people and traffic were moving too fast. I imagined how it must feel to someone who had been locked away for years.

Over the next few hours I gradually became re-accustomed to all of this and at the end of the day we drove to Brighton beach, where we sat in the car and watched the sun go down. It was just mum and me, the woman who had not only brought me into the world, but who had fought so hard to keep me here. A Lou Reed song played on the radio, "Perfect Day".

The day was 'perfect' with my mum by my side. She had been through all of this with me and as the song infers, I certainly was paying the price for my choices.

What timing, I was alive! After all I'd been through, I was still here to enjoy another magnificent sunset and as I listened to the lyrics, my heart welled up with emotion. I still get goose bumps when I hear that song.

Mum didn't once mention the drugs or how I got sick. She didn't need to. We both knew. She was just there for me. Despite what she may have been feeling, she showed me unconditional love and that was just what I needed.

What I put my parents through back then, I can only imagine. Through all of this they were both working full time in the family business. My mum showed a love that still amazes me. I know that she couldn't stand the thought of losing her only daughter. When her mother was sick, also in the Alfred Hospital, mum had visited her every day and on the one day that she wasn't able to go, my Nan died. Throughout my long stay in hospital, mum visited me every day and the one day that she rang in to say she was too sick to come in, was the day that I fell into the coma. Mum never missed a day again.

Although I had no doubt that my dad loved me, he didn't handle the whole thing very well. He was totally shocked that I had been using drugs and so disappointed with me. I guess he had to deal with his own feelings and all of this while still trying to keep the business running.

11

Maternal Instincts

I spent almost five months in hospital and finally left with a strong heart but still only forty percent function in both kidneys. By this time something new had begun to dawn on me. After all that my body had been through, I began to realise that I had probably ruined my chances of ever becoming a mother and I asked my doctors about this continually, hoping that they would say that everything would be alright. However, that was not the case. Some doctors just tried to change the subject while others were more forthright and said that I should do my best to make the most of what health I had left.

Prior to all of this, David R and I had been living together and after a few months out of hospital I moved back in with him. Unintentionally, about eight months later, I fell pregnant. I went to my doctor and he stressed, that with only forty percent kidney function and with so much damage to my whole arterial system, it would not be possible for me to successfully carry a child. A pregnancy would probably kill me. If I did survive the baby probably would not. On his recommendation I had my pregnancy terminated.

This nearly destroyed me. At birth I had been blessed with a strong, healthy body and now, because of my own stupidity, I had seemingly ruined any chance of becoming a mother. I fought back tears for days as I tried to get my head around all of this, while my heart ached for the child I had lost. The regret that I now felt for having terminated that first pregnancy, when I had been perfectly healthy, was almost unbearable. It felt as though I was being punished.

But that was not the end of the story. About ten months later, once again I fell pregnant. Again my doctor told me that the risks were far too great, and recommended that I terminate the pregnancy. This time I could not. I decided that the emotional pain was too much, so whatever the risk, I would continue with this pregnancy. At this point David R and I were married. The prayers continued for me and things went well until, as predicted by my doctors, my kidneys began to fail. I was 34 weeks pregnant (six weeks early). I had an emergency caesarean section and our beautiful son Kyle was born. It was touch and go for him for a while, but we both survived. My obstetrician, Professor Bill Walters, who delivered Kyle, performed a vertical incision (rather than the more common horizontal incision) so that he could look directly at my kidneys from the inside. The report from this confirmed the results of previous tests. Professor Walters said that both of my kidneys were so small and scarred that I would need a transplant one day.

CR

During my stay in the maternity ward, I witnessed the unfolding of another really sad drug-related story. When I was 27 weeks pregnant with Kyle I went into premature labour. The doctors managed to halt this with drugs, but given my massive medical history, they decided not to take any chances and put me into hospital to rest until my delivery. I was admitted to the maternity ward in the Queen Victoria Hospital, Melbourne. The ward was a huge, long room with about twenty beds and an adjoining veranda with another six. This ward was filled with women with all types of high risk pregnancies. In particular there were a number who were there because of drug dependence. Jess was one of these women. She was a very likable girl with a family who adored her but she had an out-of-control heroin addiction. She was on methadone but still could not help herself. Apparently her family had tried everything.

Jess was allowed to leave the hospital occasionally. One night when she was about eight and a half months pregnant she was caught on camera on Fitzroy Street, St. Kilda, soliciting. This was aired on Mike Willesee's Current Affair. She had told the reporters that she was trying to make money to buy clothes for her baby. But we all knew that this was not the case as her mother was to have custody of her baby. When Jess' baby boy was born, she gave him the nick-name E.T. This was because, as a result of her addiction, his skin was too big for his body and he looked very wrinkly.

Two years later there was another report on Mike Willesee. Jess' baby boy was now a cute little blonde toddler but the report was not about him. Sadly, Jess had fallen asleep while smoking a cigarette and died when the house she was in burned down. One of the side-effects of heroin is that it causes the user to nod-off. I have no doubt that this is probably what happened to Jess, causing her to drop her cigarette and set the house on fire. Another precious life wasted because of the evil force of drugs!

12

Hope

When Kyle was 13 months old, although I knew it was foolish, I began to feel incomplete with only one child. I still had only forty percent function of both kidneys. If my kidneys were to completely fail in another pregnancy and I was to die, I would leave my precious son without a mother. Brian, who had stayed in touch with me, had invited me a few times to have prayer at a 'miracle meeting' held at the Dandenong Town Hall. I had always thought that this was not for me, but now I was desperate and beginning to hope that maybe there could be a God and just maybe He could help me. So I contacted Brian and he took me along to a meeting that week. I had no intention at all of becoming a Christian and I was certainly not going to make a scene. The last time that I had been in a church was at my brother's wedding, four years earlier when I had been on speed. (I hadn't intended to do that. It was just that the previous night David R and I had had some speed and it left us both so wiped out the next day that we wouldn't have made it to the wedding without it.)

At this point I'd just like to add, Brian was the Hampton Baptist Minister and the meeting he took me to in Dandenong, was run by South Eastern Christian Centre, from Endeavour Hills and nobody there knew us or my medical history.

I will never forget what happened that day. A Pastor named Nancy Harkin shared her story of how she'd had heart and kidney failure and how God had healed her! I felt numb as I listened to her words. It seemed like someone was pointing straight at me. I knew that I was meant to be there that day and nervously, I went up the front for prayer. I poured out my problems to Nancy and she laid her hand on me and began to pray. I felt something so powerful touch me from the inside that I burst into tears and wept and sobbed. So much for not making a scene! But I had felt the 'Touch of the Master's hand'! It was as if some giant, loving hand was reaching down into the depths of my heart and pulling out all of the pain that I had pushed down over the past few years. The babies I had lost, the premature birth of Kyle, the health I had lost, the constant bad news I had heard about my future and the massive sense of regret that I felt. This all came out in a gush of tears that now gave me such a sense of relief and peace. I hadn't really cried for years. I had walked into that building one person and after an unmistakable touch of God, I walked out another; my life forever changed. That was the day, the 17th July 1985, I chose Jesus to be my Lord and Saviour. ☺

☙

You know, God is SO Amazing. I didn't really know any Christians apart from my brother, and he went to a church full of older people, who were lovely I'm sure, but not for me. My friends were still using drugs and partying. I must have filled out a contact card at that Miracle Meeting because about a week later I received a call from a man from South Eastern Christian Centre. He asked me if I knew two guys named Steve and Chris Jamieson to which I replied, "Pardon?" He asked again and I said "How do you know them?" You see, the last time I had known these guys, they had been using and dealing heroin. How could this Christian possibly know them? He replied, "They have been coming to our church for about a year now". I couldn't believe my ears. Chris' wife, Julie, then contacted me and I began to attend their church and also joined their Bible study group. It was as though God had lined up someone I could relate to, someone who had also been through the drug scene. Without this I would probably never have gone to a church. My journey with Jesus began.

Over the next few weeks, following the prayer, I had further kidney function tests and for the first time in three years they began to improve. This improvement continued until my kidney function was just within the normal range. Two years later I gave birth to our second beautiful son Stefan. Once again my doctors had warned me of the risks and again, suggested that I consider a termination, but this time I had no kidney failure. In fact, the report that followed the second inspection of my kidneys, during that caesarean section, was this... "This is amazing. Both Kidneys are now larger, of normal texture and like 'new' kidneys compared with their appearance three years earlier." That news was awesome, as scar tissue doesn't heal! That is why we have such long waiting lists for kidney transplants. Three years later we were blessed with yet another beautiful gift, Phoebe, and all three children were born fit and healthy and have remained so ever since.

At the time of writing, Kyle is 24 and is a fully qualified diesel mechanic. He is a youth leader at the Berwick Church of Christ and has a real heart for young people who are struggling with life. He mentors a few young teenage boys who are just working their way through the trials of life. He takes them fishing, snorkelling or just hangs out with them, working on cars or watching movies.

Stefan is 22, was dux at Hillcrest Christian College in 2005 and has just completed his Bachelor of Science at Monash University, Clayton. He is a talented musician, with the gift of a beautiful singing voice and has been very involved in the youth and adult music ministry at the Winepress (Berwick Assembly Of God - AOG.). Stefan has just moved to Japan to spend 12 months there, teaching English.

Phoebe is 19 and is our precious baby. Having completed her VCE, she has a beautiful heart for others, attends the Winepress youth group and is just working her way through the teenage years. Phoebe is currently studying a TAFE course in Events Management.

In light of my past, the gift of these three amazing children has made me feel that I am the most blessed woman on this planet. I know that when God healed me, He could see beyond me and even beyond my children, for his plans are far greater than any we could ever dream of.

> *"For I know the plans I have for you,"* declares the Lord, *"plans to prosper you and not to harm you, plans to give you a hope and a future."*
> Jeremiah 29:11

13

The Journey

My walk with Jesus has been quite a journey. As I learned more about God and acknowledged just how sick I had been, I finally recognised His hand on my life. I had been under the care of the top Professors and specialists at the Alfred Hospital, one of Melbourne's most advanced hospitals and although they tried many different drugs in an attempt to cure me, everything had pointed to the fact that I had absolutely no chance of survival at all. It was just too late!

I was only 25 years old. I should have been in the prime of my life, with a future full of hopes and dreams. Dreams of children, grandchildren and one day wonderful memories of a long life, well lived. But there I was, on the verge of surrendering all of that to the clutches of death. And where to from there? I had rejected God, whom the Bible describes as Love personified. Because of my choice, I was destined to spend an eternity alone, without God, in a place apart from Him; in other words, a place without love. But the desperate prayers for me continued and in answer to those prayers, Jesus reached down and took my hand and pulled me back. Although I did not deserve it, at the very last minute, He gave me another chance. To be so close to eternal darkness and yet to be redeemed really does something to you.

"For He has rescued us from the dominion of darkness and brought us into the kingdom of the Son He loves, in whom we have redemption, the forgiveness of sins."
Colossians 1:13-14

Whenever I think of just what Jesus did for me, my heart wells up with love and gratitude for Him.

"So Christ was sacrificed once to take away the sins of many people."
Hebrews 9:28a

To think that Jesus took my sins upon himself, when He suffered on the cross, that I might be set free from eternal darkness, just blows my mind.

These days many people think that Jesus was some wimpy guy who lived 2000 years ago. They imagine that to believe in Him means to leave fun behind and become some kind of goody, goody. WRONG! To come to know Jesus through prayer, the local church and His word, (the Bible) is to begin a powerful, enlightening spiritual walk; one that leaves me wondering, how I possibly existed without Him beforehand. A world famous hymn expresses this better than I possibly can:

Amazing Grace
"Amazing Grace, how sweet the sound,
That saved a wretch like me -
I once was lost, but now I'm found.
Was blind, but now I see"...
I was lost and blind, but now, by the grace of God, I can see.

It's as if there is a line between belief in Jesus and unbelief. Until you take that step of faith, and ask Jesus to come into your heart, you cannot see! Once you take that step the awesome spiritual world God has designed for us all, begins to unfold. This invitation is open to everyone.

"For God so loved the world that He gave his only Son that whoever believes in Him shall not perish, but have eternal life. For God did not send His Son into the world to condemn the world, but to save the world through Him. Whoever believes in Him is not condemned, but whoever does not believe stands condemned already."

Jesus ... John 3:16-18a

"He who has an ear, let him hear what the Spirit says to the churches. To him who overcomes, I will give the right to eat from the tree of life, which is in the paradise of God."

Jesus ... Revelation 2:7

14

The Battle

In the years since then I have had many wonderful times and blessings but there has also been another side. Because of my past and God's amazing grace toward me, I have always had an overwhelming desire to share my story and give glory to God. As a result of this I have often found myself a target of God's adversary...Satan!

In this world I'm sure most would acknowledge the presence of what we might call good and evil / light and dark or even the positive and negative side to life. I refer to the Bible when I describe the source behind these polar opposites. That is God (or Jesus) and Satan (or the Devil); call it what you will, but the following story refers to this source of evil.

The first hint that Satan was targeting me began in the form of unprovoked panic attacks. I had never had any such attacks in my life, not even throughout all of my illness, but soon after turning to Jesus, they began. One evening, when I was a very young Christian I was driving along Heatherton Road to church (which at that time was held at the Doveton High School Hall), when out of the blue one of these panic attacks came on. I was suddenly gripped with fear, my heart pounding as I struggled to breathe. You see, he –Satan – had a foothold. Because of my previous heart and kidney failure and seizures, etc, the voice in my head told me that I was going to have a heart attack or seizure and black out and hit a light pole or tree, killing my baby, Kyle, who was in the car with me. I pulled over, got out of the car and walked around, trying to calm down. Everything inside of me wanted to turn the car around and flee back home. But I had learnt just enough about spiritual matters to realise that if I did this, I would never be able to walk into church again. The fear (Satan) would have won! So with all the courage I could muster, I got back into my car and continued on to church. By the time I made it to the car park, my heart felt as though it would burst right out of my chest. I packed Kyle quickly into his pram and headed for the door. Then an amazing thing happened!! The moment I walked through that door, "he" fled. The fear completely disintegrated!

That was the first time I personally came to recognise the power of God over the devil. There were a few more panic attacks, which usually occurred as I was doing something involving church, and I very soon learned the power of the Name of JESUS! In the middle of an attack, when the irrational fear was so great that I could not even speak, I just repeated the name of Jesus over and over in my head, and because of His Name, Satan had to flee!

It's been a long time since "he" has tried that one on me...Praise God! But let me tell you "he" never completely gives up. Recently, while contemplating writing my story, I had another similar experience, something I had only experienced one other time since I had become a Christian. In the middle of the night, when I was in a deep sleep, I suddenly felt a crushing weight on my entire body. It also seemed as though a giant hand was pressing over my mouth and nose, blocking my breathing. I have been a Christian for 24 years now and even in my sleep, in my mind I knew I had to cry out to Jesus. I fought and fought to get his name out and finally I did. Instantly I was set free. In shock, I reached out to turn on the light but then realised that I need not fear as Jesus had protected me again. I lay there in the dark and took stock of what had just happened. This had not been sleep apnoea or any breathing related problem. I was cool and lying comfortably on my side, my mouth closed and breathing through my nose, with a totally clear airway.

This had definitely been a spiritual attack; an attack from the one who comes to take away our hope. Praise God for the name of His Son - Jesus.

"The thief comes only to steal and kill and destroy;
I have come that they may have life and have it to
the full."
Jesus   ....John 10 :10

(By the completion of writing I had suffered a total of three such attacks. Although the scenarios were different all of these occurred in the middle of the night while I was sound asleep and each responded instantly to the name of Jesus.)

"Therefore God exalted him to the highest place
and gave him the name that is above every name,
that at the name of Jesus every knee should bow,
in heaven and on earth and under the earth, and
every tongue confess that Jesus Christ is Lord."
Philippians 2:9-11

I acknowledge that not everyone would comprehend my spiritual experiences. However, I also recognise that people are looking for answers to this life through many different spiritual avenues. On a recent Melbourne television programme, I watched as a spiritual medium supposedly spoke to the dead relatives of people in the audience. The camera scanned around, showing the faces of the audience and everyone was mesmerised, hanging off the medium's every word. They were asking questions about their dead loved ones and without question, accepting the obscure comments from the medium. Yet many think there is something wrong with those who say that they have a personal relationship with God! People need answers. We are spiritual beings living in a physical world and it has been said that each one of us has a God-shaped hole in our heart that God alone can fill. The New Age movement is full of people the world over, seeking many different spiritual pathways in an attempt to fill this void. We need only ask anyone involved in witchcraft or Wicca, to find that there is definitely spiritual power outside the everyday normal physical realm. However, I believe it is only when that hole is filled by God, that a person can really feel complete. I had tried to fill the void with drugs and through many other spiritual pathways such as meditation, Thai Chi and various Chinese therapies etc., but now I know that there is only one answer - Jesus!

15

Reality

I have come to accept that although Jesus heals and forgives, there can be consequences for our choices. I have been left with a small thorn in my side. As my kidney function is only just within normal (far better than the 'below five percent function' I once had), I have had to take medication since 1982. As a result, the combination of having slightly dodgy kidneys and taking this tablet has left me with some lethargy. So I have had a bit more of a struggle than I might otherwise have had, had I been totally healed. When I first chose Jesus, I asked him, "If you could restore my heart in just a few days, then why didn't you completely heal my kidneys in that week as well?"

His answer was direct and simple. If I had been completely healed in that first week in hospital, I most certainly would have got back into drugs. There was one time after all of my illness (before my children were born) when I begged a friend to give me some heroin and eventually, he did. He left a small amount on a ledge in the kitchen of my home. I walked past it about ten times, maybe even twenty times, desperately torn between the desire to feel the rush in my vein and the fear of what might happen. The fear won and I knew that that chapter of my life was over for ever. God always knows what He is doing. He knew exactly what it would take to keep me away from drugs forever.

Recently I had another revelation which really took me by surprise. I was driving to work one morning, praying for a friend who had been struggling with a drug problem, when out of the blue I found myself in a weird place of deja-vu. I was having a flashback to the heroin days. I suddenly recalled all of the feelings I used to know so well. The craving that sets the wheels in motion; the churning of my stomach as scoring draws closer and then the powerful physical effect after the hit. But then, just as suddenly, my mind filled with the reality of the destruction all of this brings to the user; mentally, emotionally, physically and spiritually. I think God was reminding me that I am only human and over the years, with others around me still using, I could have easily succumbed to the temptation, had I not been left with some scars. Of course, I would have told myself that I was under pressure and it would only be this once. I could control it. But that is just how this insipid drug creeps in. I guess it's the same for any addiction. I thank God that he gave me what it took to overcome it.

Having said all of this, despite the lethargy, I have raised three amazing children, worked part time and, some years ago, I even got back into horse riding. So I may not have perfect health, but given my past, I cannot complain.

CR

It may seem that this all happened long ago and that not much is reported about heroin O.D.s these days. Make no mistake, heroin is still around and I guess could be called the silent killer. Some years ago, long after my illness, my dad employed a man for a few weeks to re-paint the interior of his city business. He was a handsome, fit looking young man with his whole life ahead of him. One day he asked my dad if he could have his wage a few days early as he was having a dinner party and needed the money for food. Well, food was not the only thing on the shopping list! That night his girlfriend died of a heroin overdose. As if that was not tragic enough, about eight months later we learnt of this young man's death, also from a drug overdose. Among the many death notices, there was one tragically sad notice in the obituaries from his adoring, grieving grandfather who was trying to come to terms with the pointless loss of his beloved grandson.

❦

Between school and his apprenticeship, our son Kyle had a holiday job with a young panel beater. He was a very likeable young man in his twenties and about 18 months ago we learned of his death, once again from a heroin overdose. I really grieved over the next few days as I pictured his smiling face and easy-going attitude and recalled that he had only recently been married and had a young baby.

This was a young man, who had been born into the world with so much potential. Loved and nurtured by his parents. Lovingly tended to, when as a little boy, he scraped a knee. He had journeyed through primary school, secondary school, completed an apprenticeship and started his own business. He was a young man with his whole future ahead of him until drugs entered his world and tragically robbed him of all of that.

The fact is that not everyone using drugs is an evil, dangerous criminal. Drugs of all kinds are readily available and can affect normal, everyday, hardworking people and change their lives in the most horrendous way. Just recently I came across the following article:

Sunday Herald Sun, March 22, 2009
"Fears of rise in heroin overdoses
Incidents of heroin overdose in Victoria have spiked as experts expect a global opium

```
boom to bring more of the lethal drug into
Australia.
Local paramedics have noticed a rise in
adverse reactions to the drug in the past
four months.
Their concerns come as the Australian
National Council On Drugs has warned of "new
risks for Australia" from heroin.
Figures show the amount of heroin seized in
Australia doubled in 2006-07.
During the week, Victoria Police seized more
than 700g of heroin and arrested four people
in a western suburbs drug bust..."
```

Unfortunately it seems that things will only get worse.

Over the years, I have come to recognise that there are two main categories that hard drug users fall into: there are those who are foolish and naive and just get into drugs for a bit of fun, then there are those who have some kind of emotional damage and find that opiates somehow relieve their pain. Either way, addiction usually follows. I believe it is far more difficult to escape this addiction if the motive for using drugs is emotional pain relief. I fell into the first category. David fell into the second. David did eventually choose Jesus, but without a life threatening illness, he battled with his addiction far longer than me. His story could fill another book.

As for my friend, Vicki, she did manage to get her life together and is now happily married in NSW and is still riding horses. Vicki is one of the 'lucky' ones.

Apart from Hepatitis B, I discovered some years ago (approximately 1994) that I had also contracted Hepatitis C. This is a condition that had not even been given a name in 1982, so I am not sure exactly when I contracted it, although, I did have a negative test result in 1992. The amazing thing now, is that I no longer have either Hepatitis B or Hepatitis C. In fact, in the case of the Hepatitis C, I am one of the 20% who have 'spontaneously recovered'. In other words, I have been cleared of it with no treatment at all. In the other 80% of cases, Hepatitis C is a disease that can affect the sufferer for life. Interferon treatment (which was earlier used experimentally on me), is today used regularly in an attempt to cure these patients, although I am not aware of the success rate. Apparently, it has been estimated that at this point in time, 2.2% of the world's population is infected with Hepatitis C. That is about 130 million people! The majority of these cases involve people who have been infected by using contaminated needles, for illegal drug use. Unfortunately, there are also still some incidences of infection through blood transfusions with contaminated blood.

Another amazing fact is that I no longer have any signs of Polyarteritis Nodosa; a disease that I was expected to suffer from for life!

Although I have been cleared of these three diseases, there remains one prevailing thought that stands out in my mind. The fact is that, relatively speaking, my drug years were only a very small percentage of my life and yet they have influenced the rest of my life. It is very rarely that a person enters the dark world of drug addiction and leaves it unscathed - if alive at all.

16

Conclusion

So, why me? Why did all of these things happen to me? Who else did I know who had nearly died from not one, but two extremely rare diseases? A few years ago I learnt the Bible verse in Deuteronomy 28:22 under the heading of Curses for Disobedience, *"...the Lord will strike you with wasting disease, with **'fever and inflammation'**, with scorching heat and drought, with blight and mildew which will plague you until you perish."* A chill raced down my spine as I read these words. I had nearly died from Typhoid *'**fever**'* and then five years later nearly died again from Polyarteritis Nodosa, which translated, meant that my major organs and all of my arterial system had been totally struck with '*inflammation*'.

Now I had certainly been disobedient, but without going into it, out of respect for others, I also discovered that I had a history of generational, occult activity through my life. As far as I know, those involved had been unwittingly caught up in these things, totally unaware of the darker side of them. I am not sure exactly how this works, but I do know that once we open the door into anything that goes directly against God's laws, we invite all sorts of spirits in and curses can be passed down through the generations. I have learnt that I had probably been under a curse and by the power of Jesus, I have been set free. I believe this possibly also applies to the earlier reference to Meg's mother, who had been reading the tarot cards.

> "*Let no one be found among you..... who practices divination or sorcery, interprets omens, engages in witchcraft, or casts spells or who is a medium or spiritist or who consults the dead.*"
> Deuteronomy 18:10a and 10c—11

How many other unsuspecting people out there are suffering in some way for similar reasons?

In Australia, we don't hear much about curses, except maybe in the context of a joke. However, if we lived in some parts of Africa, South America, New Guinea and probably many other places around the globe, we would understand the reality of a curse. Even the Aborigines have the "pointing the bone" which can invoke a powerful curse on the recipient, sometimes even causing death. Besides, if the Bible says curses exist, that's good enough for me.

"Our battle is not against flesh and blood, but against the powers, the principalities and the rulers of this dark world and the spiritual forces of evil in the heavenly realms"
Ephesians 6:12

But with God we do not need to fear as God is Love and His word says:

"God is Love"
1 John 4:16 b

"There is no fear in love. But perfect love drives out fear"
1 John 4:18

"So do not fear, for I am with you"
Isaiah 41:10

God truly is a God of love and it is His desire to see everyone set free from every form of bondage, whether drug or alcohol addiction, gambling, depression, sickness, occult activity or fear - when we turn to Him, through His Son Jesus, we can find this release.

I had another question for God. We hear that every day millions of people all over the world die from starvation, sickness, accidents etc, so why not me? What difference would one extra person make? Surely I was no more special to God than anyone else? And as I have said, I know that I would not have spent eternity with God as I had rejected Him! The only answer I can find is that all life is precious to God and his heart aches for all those who die without Him, but I had a few things going for me. Firstly, I had Bible-believing Christians earnestly praying for me. There is power in our prayers in the name of His son Jesus! Secondly, I'm sure that He knew that I would one day choose Him and go on to share His story in my life. I only hope that I am doing Him justice.

"I will not die, but live and proclaim what the Lord has done"
Psalm 118:17

And of course God surely has plans for my children and their children. I guess really, I am just trying my best to make sense of it all. Whenever I hear of a death from a heroin overdose, I almost carry a sense of guilt that I am still here. In truth, only God has the answer.

⌗

As I write this account we are currently in the middle of a world economic downturn with many countries heading into recession and in some cases, possibly even depression. The doom and gloom of climate change is constantly flooding media outlets. Horrific stories of terrorism are regularly splashed across the news. We have also just had an outbreak of 'Swine Flu' and the World Health Organisation has issued a stage five alert, one stage short of pandemic. The number of people clinically depressed is at an all-time high. This could be the recipe for fear and panic, but with Christ I know that I need not fear as my faith gives me a supernatural sense of peace amongst the turmoil. While I personally don't wish to die just yet (there are many things about this crazy world I do love, especially my family), like anyone else, I know that death is not entirely in my control. Life brings trials and tribulation, good times and bad to us all, but I, along with my brothers and sisters in Christ, have a reason for this sense of peace. We know that even though our bodies will eventually die, because of Christ's sacrifice and love for us, our spirit and soul will join Him and live for an eternity.

"I am the resurrection and the life. He who believes in me will live, even though he dies; and whoever lives and believes in me will never die. Do you believe this?"
Jesus . . . John 11:25

"I am the way and the truth and the life. No one comes to the Father except through me."
Jesus . . . John 14 :6

"Come to me all you who are weary and burdened, and I will give you rest. Take my yoke upon you and learn from me, for I am gentle and humble in heart, and you will find rest for your souls. For my yoke is easy and my burden is light."
Jesus... Matthew 11:28—30

As mentioned earlier this invitation is open to all of mankind.

Over the years I have become more and more aware of the Love and Grace shown to me by our Wonderful Creator. Despite all of the stupid, selfish and illegal things I have done (including abusing the healthy body God freely gave me, not to mention what I put my family through), my Saviour has forgiven me of my sins and given me a new beginning. As stated previously, I am not proud of many of the things I have done, but neither do I continue to carry the weight of shame, as He has taken that shame away. On the day that I chose to follow Jesus, He washed away my past and made me like new. I did nothing to deserve this. This is Grace. The very thought of this gives me goose bumps all over!

"Therefore if anyone is in Christ he is a new creation, the old has gone, the new has come"
2 Corinthians 5:17

Despite the dark period in my life, I am still the same optimistic, friendly, fun-loving person I always was, but spiritually I have become a new creation.

When I ponder this story it still sends a chill down my spine. To think that One so mighty, heard the prayers of so few and restored the life of one so insignificant. What an Awesome God we have.

Kerryn Redpath

*"God is **Light**; in Him there is no **Darkness** at all"*
1John 1:5B

Praise the Lord, O my soul,

And forget not all of his benefits-

Who forgives all your sins

And heals all your diseases,

Who redeems your life from the pit

And crowns you with love and

compassion

Who satisfies your desires with good

things

So that your youth is renewed like the eagle's

Psalm 103:2-5

Acknowledgements

My ever loving Mum and Dad who went through more than any parent should have to because of my stupid choices.

My brothers David and Ian for their prayers and love.

Pastor Brian McKelvie and his wife Marie, for not giving up on me and their assistance with editing.

My amazing teams of doctors, nurses, Professors and specialists, who not only used all of their brilliance and expertise, but also treated me with dignity and respect, despite my crazy behaviour.

My three beautiful children, Kyle, Stefan and Phoebe, for just being the people God created them to be.

My wonderful friends, Cathy Wieckmann, Rosalyn Dyne, Alison Leonard, Kelly Dickson, Jane Sheppard and Alex Marshall who have helped me in so many ways.

All of my close friends, who have endured my random ravings, as I have relived all of these wild memories.

Wendy Bytheway for her magical editorial touch.

And last but by no means least....

My Lord and Saviour, Jesus Christ, for His Amazing Grace.

If anyone reading my story has seen the touch of God on my life and would also like to know this same loving God, this awesome Jesus, a good place to begin, would be to say a prayer something like this:

"Father God, in the name of your Son Jesus, please forgive me for living life my way. Forgive me for anything I have ever done wrong. Jesus, I now open my heart and choose you to be my Lord and Saviour. Lord, please fill me with your Holy Spirit. Take my life and do something with it. Make my life really count. Thank you for your promise of eternal life. Amen."

After praying this, it is really important to find a local, Bible believing church and get connected, so that you can be guided and encouraged throughout your journey. You will not regret it. Having a relationship with the living, breathing Creator of the Universe, and everything in it, is indescribable.

CONCLUSION

ⳤ

If you or someone you know needs help with drug addiction, go to:

www.teenchallenge.com.au

Ph: (03) 5852 3777   (international code +61 3 5852 3777)

To connect with a good Bible believing Church within
Australia try:
Australian Christian Churches, National Office:
(02) 8853 5150.
Or internationally, try internet search
"A.O.G. - Assemblies of God"

To purchase copies of '*Out of the Darkness*' please go to:-

www.daesy.com.au